Church of Thrones

A Vision and Call for Organizing God's Kingdom on Earth

Chris Rush

…so that you would walk in a manner worthy
of the God who calls you
into His own kingdom and glory.
1 Thessalonians 2:12

I dedicate this to my queen—my wife—who has not only said "Yes" to marrying a guy like me, but to also building a family and doing the hard work of preparing for Jesus' return with me. I love you.

Most importantly, to our Father in heaven, who saw fit to adopt me and bring me into His royal family, and to His first born Son, my brother, KING Yeshua...for paying the price for me to become co-heir with Him. And finally, the Holy Spirit, for His steadfast leadership in my life.

Table of Contents

Introduction

This book is for the Church at large. In other words, this book is for the Christian. It addresses the identity of every Christian as a part of the Kingdom of God, as seen in the Scripture. It also addresses the royal posture from which we should act toward one another and the world; And how we should organize ourselves to most appropriately reflect our place in the Kingdom of God. If the content of this book is embraced, it will change the institutional expression of our Christianity and bring the church into full maturity, power and love.

The Phenomenon of "Game of Thrones"

Unless you have been living under a rock, you have at the very least heard of the HBO show *Game of Thrones*. The show has been a worldwide sensation, breaking records with millions of viewers. The show in its coming last season will spend $7 million dollars an episode. It has become a pop-culture sensation, bleeding into the way NFL teams market themselves to even parodies on the cover of construction supply magazines. Seems like you can't go anywhere without someone bringing it up. The series has received 38 Primetime Emmy Awards, including Outstanding Drama Series in 2015 and 2016, more than any other primetime scripted television series.

I've had a long-standing belief that God uses Hollywood to send a message, even when the people doing it may not realize it. In 2015, God used the film *Noah* to shout that we are living in the days of Matthew 23. I believe God wanted to let this generation know that those days are today. So, He spoke to Hollywood and they obeyed and created a film—a horrible film, yes—I never said they would fully honor Him in doing it. Nonetheless, a multi-million dollar budget was spent on making and promoting a movie called *Noah*, with billboards all around the nation stating, "We are living in the days of Noah." The prophetic word was out, and those who had an ear to hear, heard it.

I could go on and on about different films I believe God inspired to release a message. Films like *Horton Hears a Who*, *The Hobbit Series*, and *The Matrix*, just to name a few. I know God is sovereign over all things, including Hollywood. The show *Game of Thrones* is no different. This medieval-based TV drama has captivated millions, and I believe God is behind it all. But why?

Game of Thrones is one of the best pictures I have seen, outlining how the Kingdom of God, here on earth, should work in the physical absence of the King of kings—Jesus/Yeshua. With an overarching theme of honor, loyalty, family, and respect for authority, this show has many Biblical lesson takeaways, specifically with regard to how royalty should and should not act—as well as the rewards when things are done right and the cost when things are done wrong. When the Lord gave me the title for this work you are reading, I automatically understood the pun and saw the genius in it.

In light of this, I use 🔱 a king chess piece image to mark when I am making a direct connection between the *Game of Thrones*, and a Biblical truth. If you are a fan of the show, keep your eyes peeled for this chess piece as you read.

I want to be clear. If you haven't seen the show, it is not necessary to watch it to understand what I will be laying out in this book. In fact, I am not even endorsing the show. Though I believe *Game of Thrones* was inspired by God, the show is not holy and should not be viewed by everyone. Namely, there is a significant amount of nudity in the show. So much so, I felt the Lord convicting me about watching it. Instead, I opted to watch YouTube videos recapping episodes, instead of watching the whole thing. That way, I would know what was going on, without being exposed to all the things that make my flesh stir.

In short, you do not have to be a fan to appreciate the connection. The Lord has given me a picture of how He desires the church to function and be organized. I see it affirmed in Scripture, and in many ways, symbolized in *Game of Thrones*. I fully believe that before His return, and through one generation, God will redefine our institutionalized way of doing Christianity. I believe that what I outline in this book is what it will look like. My hope is, by the end of this book, you will see how the church is in fact, a "Church of Thrones".

Chapter One
The God of Royalty

To begin our journey, we first must lay out the amazing truth that God himself is a royal God. And He desires to build for Himself a royal family. There is no shortage of Scripture for both points. The Bible is clear.

The Lord has established His throne in heaven, And His kingdom rules over all. (Psalms 103:19)

For I know that the Lord is great, And our Lord is above all gods. Whatever the Lord pleases He does, in heaven and in earth. (Psalms 135: 5-6)

The Lord is in His holy temple, The Lord's throne is in heaven; His eyes behold, His eyelids test the sons of men. (Psalms 11:4)

9

Heaven is My throne, And earth is My footstool. "What house will you build for Me?" says the Lord, "Or what is the place of My rest?" (Acts 7:49)

Immediately I was in the Spirit; and behold, a throne set in heaven, and One sat on the throne. (Revelation 4:2)

Then Micah said, "Therefore hear the word of the Lord: I saw the Lord sitting on His throne, and all the host of heaven standing by, on His right hand and on His left." (1 Kings 22:19)

In the year that King Uzziah died, I saw the Lord sitting on a throne, high and lifted up, and the train of His robe filled the temple. (Isaiah 6:1)

Now this is the main point of the things we are saying: We have such a High Priest, who is seated at the right hand of the throne of the Majesty in the heavens... (Hebrews 8:1)

He comes from the north as golden splendor; With God is awesome majesty. (Job 37:22)

I watched till thrones were put in place, And the Ancient of Days was seated; His garment was white as snow, And the hair of His head was like pure wool. His throne was a fiery flame, Its wheels a burning fire..." (Daniel 7:9)

Whenever the living creatures give glory and honor and thanks to Him who sits on the throne, who lives forever and ever... (Revelation 4:9)

But I say to you, do not swear at all: neither by heaven, for it is God's throne... (Matthew 5:34)

Then I saw a great white throne and Him who sat on it, from whose face the earth and the heaven fled away... (Revelation 20:11)

Then I looked, and I heard around the throne and the living creatures and the elders the voice of many angels, numbering myriads of myriads and thousands of thousands, saying with a loud voice, "Worthy is the Lamb who was slain, to receive power and wealth and wisdom and might and honor and glory and blessing!" (Revelation 5:11-12)

The Bible is filled with the consistent reminder that the Lord God created all things and is a King who sits on the throne above all things. There is none like Him. He raises earthly kings up and tears them down. He is supreme over all things. He is the undefeated champion of the generations—He stands only. There is no one that can compare to Him. As you see in some of these verses, He is sitting on a throne and has ten thousand, times ten thousands attending Him every moment, and many more standing before Him. He is high above the earth and the heavens. He is all-knowing, all-powerful and He is everywhere at once. He sees all things; He hears all things, even the thoughts of man. He never grows tired of holding all things together— never gets weary, impatient or worried.

He has beasts around His throne that cry out to him "holy!" These beasts have eyes all around them and inside of them; with every blink of their eye/s they are seeing a revelation of who He is that the other one has not seen—even though they have been around His throne for thousands of years! They never want to leave because within Him is total satisfaction, pleasure, joy and comfort. He is high and lifted. He is unstoppable. He never has to ask for permission—He is the boss, the King. And He is not asking for a vote on it. God in heaven is and will soon reign openly. To question His supremacy is foolish, and to rebel against His will is putting your eternal existence in a dangerous place. If you don't believe me, the First Testament is the literal history of what happens, when God's chosen people decide to throw off God's kingship and their royal call to be a nation that represent him.

Your Royal Position

Based on this Scriptural caricature of God, how should we relate to Him? How are we to approach this awesome One? Thanks be to Yeshua! He made a way for us to come to Him and His way, is Jesus. Jesus has washed us clean from sin by taking our punishment on the cross (1 Peter 3:18). For those who trust in the death and resurrection of Jesus and surrender their lives to Him (Romans 10:9), He has made them children of God (Galatians 3:26; 1 John 3:1), by making them born again by the Spirit (John 3; Ephesians 1:13), into the household of Saints (Ephesians 2:19). Because of this child/saint position, we are supposed to come to Jesus, as a child goes to their loving Father. This is amazing! He wants us to come to Him! Each one of us can know we are His

> To question His supremacy is foolish, and to rebel against His will is putting your eternal existence in a dangerous place.

favorite: confident that He loves us, because He is our Papa.

My sons never ask if they can sit on my lap—they just come and sit. And most of the time, they jump on me. This is how comfortable we should be (and even more) with our Heavenly Father. Yet and still, our Father is KING. We must never forget our Father is the Ruler of all things and with that knowledge, we speak to Him with the honor, respect and confidence due a King, while never leaving our position as his favorite child. Now if Jesus is high and lifted up over every created thing, seen and unseen (Colossians 1:17; Ephesians

13

1:23); If He is my majesty, holy, pure, the most powerful, most beautiful, and most amazing, and I am His son or daughter— then how should I speak about myself?

There has been a long-standing language and attitude among protestant Christians that is partial to identification with being sinner, but not with being a saint. Language like, "I'm just a sinner saved by grace" or "I am the chief of sinners." This is in reference to the Apostle Paul's identity claim throughout his letters. But we fail to see how Paul's language throughout his letters, blow-horns his new birthright in Christ Jesus and speaks to his sinner status as past tense.

> I thank him who has given me strength, Christ Jesus our Lord, because he judged me faithful, appointing me to his service though formerly I was a blasphemer, persecutor, and insolent opponent. But I received mercy because I had acted ignorantly in unbelief, and the grace of our Lord overflowed for me with the faith and love that are in Christ Jesus. The saying is trustworthy and deserving of full acceptance, that Christ Jesus came into the world to save sinners, of whom I am the foremost. But I received mercy for this reason, that in me, as the foremost, Jesus Christ might display his perfect patience as an example to those who were to believe in him for eternal life. To the King of the ages, immortal, invisible, the only God, be honor

and glory forever and ever. Amen. (1 Timothy 1:12-17)

As children of God, we are now acceptable and appointed to the service of the "King of kings." The way to more fully express our gospel identity, is to say something like "I WAS a sinner, saved by grace." Once you have been saved, you are not to identify yourself as a sinner, but a saint, who has been adopted by the one true God. You are now an heir of the King: chosen, holy and royal.

But you are a chosen people, a royal priesthood, a holy nation, God's special possession, that you may declare the praises of him who called you out of darkness into his wonderful light. (1 Peter 1:9)

Father God has lifted you high. Peter says your new identity is, "Chosen". "Royal". "Holy". "God's possession."

In him we were also chosen, having been predestined according to the plan of him who works out everything in conformity with the purpose of his will, in order that we, who were the first to put our hope in Christ, might be for the praise of his glory. And you also were included in Christ when you heard the message of truth, the gospel of your salvation. When you believed, you were marked in him with a seal, the promised Holy Spirit, who is a deposit guaranteeing our

15

inheritance until the redemption of those who are God's possession—to the praise of his glory. (Ephesians 1:11-15)

When a king puts a seal on something, it is irrevocable. Paul says in the Scripture above, He has put His seal on you! Your status is irrevocable. So you were a sinner—yes. You were an enemy of the one and true God—yes. But God...

But God, being rich in mercy, because of the great love with which he loved us, even when we were dead in our trespasses, made us alive together with Christ—by grace you have been saved— and raised us up with him and seated us with him in the heavenly places in Christ Jesus, so that in the coming ages he might show the immeasurable riches of his grace in kindness toward us in Christ Jesus. (Ephesians 2:4-7)

In His mercy, He raised you and seated you with Him on His throne. You are made like the SON—perfect and beloved by Him, over everything else.

Here is the truth: If you have surrendered your life to Yeshua, then He has given you His Holy Spirit—you are now royalty, true royalty. He has not only brought you into an eternal everlasting kingdom but has given you the most powerful position = Child of the King. The whole of heaven's resources are now at your whim.

If He who did not spare his own Son but gave him up for us all, how will he not also with him graciously give us all things? (Romans 8:32)

Your earthly and heavenly inheritance has been so upgraded, it can't get any better. The Most High has seated you next to Him and has given you a throne. Now it is time you take a seat in it and begin to learn how to rightly rule from that place. Once again, there is no shortage of Scripture verses illuminating this very point—that we are the royalty of heaven.

You shall also be a crown of glory In the hand of the Lord, And a royal diadem In the hand of your God. (Isaiah 62:3)

As for the saints who *are* on the earth, 'They are the excellent ones, in whom is all my delight'. (Psalm 16:3)

I love Psalm 16:3 in particular, because this verse is quoting the Lord Himself and He is calling us "excellent ones", and this phrase is typically applied to nobles, princes or chiefs (Albert Barnes, Commentary, 1870) Just like we call Him "the King" or "The Excellent One", He calls us by His own royal title. He tops it off with "...in whom is all my delight." In the Greek, this "all" means the entirety of Him. Can you imagine the entirety of God delighting in you? It may seem too good to be true; but we should trust Him at His Word.

In the natural way of royalty, it comes by blood heritage and is connected to another who holds some degree of nobility. But when it comes to God's kingdom, you are chosen and bought by royal blood from Yeshua. In result, you are a royal priesthood. Not just a priesthood, but a royal one…and not just a royal one, but the high station of royalty. In fact, Revelation 1: 5-6 clarifies, that through the blood of Jesus, we are made kings and priests,

> To Him who loved us and washed us from our sins in His own blood, and has made us kings and priests to His God and Father, to Him *be* glory and dominion forever and ever. Amen. (Revelation 1:5-6)

We must remember that our position in the Messiah did not come cheap: Yeshua paid with His own blood to make you a king and priest. Jesus is the King of kings, and in fulfilling His destiny of ruling the nations and increasing His government forever, He wants to do it with his royally purchased family—His brothers and sisters, the smaller kings and queens, forever. Because it cost His life, to turn us from common nobodies, to high rulers, I would say it's important that we walk in this fullness. The full truth, is that as royalty, we can draw near to our High Priest in His holiness. We have full access to Him—without measure—and no created being can make that claim but us.

He raises the poor out of the dust, And lifts the needy out of the ash heap, That He may seat him with princes—With the princes of His people. (Psalm 113: 7-8)

Our God is Father King, who walks the streets of the slums, chooses the needy, raises them from a dead and poor situation, brings them into the kingdom of God through faith in Jesus and His work on the cross. In this kingdom, we are not servants—He gives us a seat, a throne, next to His other children. He lets us share in His authority. This is inconceivable! It feels wrong in so many ways, but never the less true and right. Will you take Him at His Word?

> The full truth, is that as royalty, we can draw near to our High Priest in His holiness. We have full access to Him— without measure—and no created being can make that claim

When you sit and talk with the other princes and princesses, Christ followers, you find out that all but One (Jesus Himself), was bought from the slums to sit in this glorious place. In the natural sense of royalty, a baby born from a queen and king is automatically given all the rights to their father's kingdom—without question. Likewise, spiritually, when we receive Yeshua as our Messiah we are now born of a new spirit and all the rights and privileges come to us. Will you take hold of your privileges?

For through him we both have access in one Spirit to the Father. So then you are no longer strangers and aliens, but you are fellow citizens with the saints and members of the household of God, built on the foundation of the apostles and prophets, Christ Jesus himself being the cornerstone, in whom the whole structure, being joined together, grows into a holy temple in the Lord. In him you also are being built together into a dwelling place for God by the Spirit. (Ephesians 2:18-22)

I hope I have made the point that you are not average. You are not common. You have been made to be the aristocracy of the cosmos, with access to unlimited resources and power. What could be better?

Know You Are the King's Child

Years ago, my wife and I went to go see the movie X-men. At work the next day I found myself trying to move chairs without touching them. As a grown man, I secretly wished I had power, like I saw in the movie, to move objects. In this, I heard the voice of God say, "Why would you want to move a chair, when you can move my heart?" Whoa. This is profound. Who can move the One who gives strength to all (Acts 17:28)? Who has established the earth and created suns yet and still, it was made clear to me that I

> You have been made to be the aristocracy of the cosmos...

have the power to move His heart, and when His heart is moved, His actions will follow (John 11:33-44).

Many scholars believe Song of Songs is a metaphorical love story between God and His chosen people, Israel. In it, God says to His beloved, "Turn your eyes away from me they have overcome me" (Song of Sol 6:5). Do you understand what this is saying? We can overwhelm the emotion of God with our gazing on Him! Essentially, "I can't take it, look away!" As His chosen—blood-bought in Jesus—we are perfect and loved in His sight. When you look at your Father and desire to see Him clearly for who He is, He is so moved by you! He is a Father, who when you meet Him eye-to-eye, He loses it! We hear this same response echoed in the symbolic pleasure given Esther by King Ahaseurus, or Herodius' daughter by King Herod, "What do you want? I will give it to you. Even if it is half my Kingdom!"

You move to a whole different place, when you begin to live your life from this position— when you connect with the truth of who you are as royalty and how you move God because He loves you so much. Take hold of this truth, prince and princess, never let it go.

Translate Knowledge to Words

Full disclosure: I envision the worldwide Church increasing in the knowledge of ourselves as a kingdom people, so deeply, that it affects our language. In a very particular way, this has happened for me.

I work at a warehouse, and by God's grace, I work with other believers. Some that have given their life to

Christ through my witness. In our hours together, I shared this revelation of our being royal sons. It seemed only right, to then begin addressing my fellow Christian brothers at work with royal titles. Ben and Michael and Derek soon became "Your grace", "my Lord", "prince" or "your majesty". At first, it was met with clear reluctance. But over time, it took hold. We began to experience many more believing brothers strengthened, once we began calling them by their royal titles.

When the few of us first began adjusting our vocab this way, it felt weird. But only as much as it was refreshing. It soon became a powerful reminder of who we are, even in the middle of a sometimes stressful work day. Every time a brother would say "king Chris" or "Your grace", it blessed and honored me—not in a self-glorifying way, but because it pointed me to the glory of the King I belonged to. *Yes, I am a child of the king,* it would remind me. This language continues to help me live up to my position in Christ, even at work, when I can easily forget to walk in "a manner worthy of the God who calls [me] into his kingdom and glory" (1 Thessalonians 2:12).

Proud Language, Humble People

This new language is meant as a mutual blessing, for both the giver and the receiver. It blesses me to call other believers by their title, as much as it is to receive it. It reminds me that I get to hang out with royal sons of God. Both extending the title, and receiving it, is a mutual act of humility.

This may seem confusing, when these titles land on many as provocatively proud. Here is why I say using royal titles is an act of humility. To speak to one as if they are a king, you run the risk, that they won't return the gesture. Or, you run the risk that in extending the blessing, the brother or sister will reject it with false humility, saying things like, "I'm just a brother or I'm just a sinner…". They are slow to connect that these royal names are true of them, because of Jesus. I remember when a new guy started at the warehouse. I discovered he was with the Christian organization, Youth With A Mission (YWAM), so I greeted him as "your highness". He responded, "Whoa brother. I'm just a sinner saved by grace." I smiled and proceeded to ask him, "Is your father King of heaven?" He answered, "Yes." I continued, "And does He have 10,000 X 10,000 angels attending him at this moment?" He answered, "Yes." "Your highness, I can't treat you as common then" I said. As a redeemed people, I believe we are much like this guy. We are so used to hearing the watering down of our identity—half of the whole—that we no longer connect with it at all.

In contrast, my wife has taken up her identity as queen. She waitresses part time and one day her coworkers decided to divvy out nicknames for the staff. When she tells it, I imagine her rising and shining… but she says, she simply interrupted their suggestions and said, "I am a queen. I don't do nicknames." This simple act opened up a discussion as to why she felt she was a queen. It was the perfect opportunity and segue to talk about how God is King and Father—and in Christ's adoption—He makes us royal.

Another time, she experienced an incredibly rude customer. Her co-workers were upset with how the customer treated her, but my wife told them "I'm not going to let them remove me from my queendom." Impressed with her response, she established her reputation among the team as a queen. My wife understands, that in Christ we are destined to rule and reign in the heavens, and that status begins here on earth, in the place where we are. When we live like this, God increases in those spaces—even at work.

Remember the YWAM guy? My coworkers would tell me how uncomfortable my language was making him. I never will forget when that very same guy came to me, struggling with a sin failure. I began reminding him what I had been telling him, "You are a royal son of the King."

> …in Christ we are destined to rule and reign in the heavens, and that status begins here on earth, in the place where we are. When we live like this, God increases in those spaces—even at work.

The King became the lifter of his head. It was this very language that helped him out of funk and shame. And in doing this, I actually gave him a heart to share this truth with another struggling brother. So many things get solved when we know who we are! And that work will be done more speedily when we begin operating like we are in fact, in a kingdom culture.

In season one of Game of Thrones, Daenerys and her brother make plans to go back to Westeros and take back their father's throne, even though they left as children and don't remember anything of Kings landing, they both have a sense of entitlement to the whole country and will do whatever is necessary to get there. In light of this confidence, by-watchers who support Daenarys begin to stand with them in taking back the throne. This exemplifies how we should be standing regarding our birthright in Christ. We are born again. We are given the keys of heaven. We have been promised all things and we have been given the mantle to make disciples of all nations and to increase God's kingdom in every sphere. If we take the promises of our birthright and set our hearts to live out our destiny, many will come to support it, like they did in the case of Daenerys. Know, that if you set your heart to live out God's destiny for you, the devil and his hordes will not take that threat lightly. Evil will see to delay or stop you if possible. Like in GOT, you may have to go through fire and six seasons of drama before you start sailing into your destiny with 10,000 ships behind you, but if you trust in God and rely on His leadership, you can never fail.

Chapter Two

A Kingdom Culture

> [Jesus] said to them, "But who do you say
> that I am?" Simon Peter answered and said,
> "You are the Christ, the Son of the living God."
> Jesus answered and said to him, "Blessed are
> you, Simon Bar-Jonah, for flesh and blood has
> not revealed this to you, but My Father who is in
> heaven. And I also say to you that you are Peter,
> and on this rock I will build My church, and the
> gates of Hades shall not prevail against it. And I
> will give you the keys of the kingdom of heaven,
> and whatever you bind on earth will be bound in
> heaven, and whatever you loose on earth will be
> loosed in heaven." (Matthew 16:15-19)

When Jesus poses this question to the disciples,
Peter speaks up and says, "You are the Christ, the son
of the Living God." Then Jesus calls Peter the "rock" on
which He will build His church. Peter's proclamation of
who Jesus is, was the foundation for his call. This

pattern is true for us today: when we acknowledge Christ as the one and true Son of God who saves the world, then the building can begin. When Jesus says He will build His church, we can rest assure that, that is still happening. He is building, through us, until we are in perfect unity with Him, walking in perfect power, not lacking anything.

Ecclesia: The Church

What is the definition of church? The root word for church in the Greek is "ecclesia". The word ecclesia is a depiction of a ruling class of people; a group of noblemen and ladies, the leaders of a society. Webster dictionary puts it this way " : a political assembly of citizens of ancient Greek states; *especially* : the periodic meeting of the Athenian citizens for conducting public business and for considering affairs proposed by the council" (Webster, 2019)

> The word Ecclesia is a depiction of a ruling class of people; a group of noblemen and ladies, the leaders of a society.

We are not some building on the corner with people who just do good works. If this were the case, there would be no difference then, between the church and community centers. But God says, we are His ruling people, who have the power to shut and open, build and tear down. Yeshua said it himself in Matthew 16:19, "And I will give you the keys of the kingdom of heaven, and whatever you bind on earth will be bound in heaven, whatever you loose on earth will be loosed in heaven." This is almost unbelievable! God is saying He has given His church—His Ecclesia, His assembly of believers who conduct his business—the keys to the Kingdom. We have access to open up the heavens and to get what we need and bring it to earth. There is so much modern teaching on this very concept of binding and loosing, but the short and sweet version is: you rule. You have been given authority to take whatever is on the earth that is contrary to the kingdom of God and bind it with word and action. When you do this, heaven will back you up. Likewise, you can request what is good from heaven and move it to be loosed here on the earth. The gates of hell will not prevail against the ruling people. In other words, no barrier that the enemy puts up will win in the end. The church is a courtroom of noble princes and princesses who influence all the earth for righteousness sake. When you see the word "Church", I suggest, you start seeing the word: Ecclesia.

According to the model the Romans set, the ecclesia consisted of other rulers in the land. Every king would have a throne room, and that room was also known as the courtroom, where all the nobles met with each other to do business for the Kingdom, or participate and witness important matters with the King. The activities of a courtroom would vary day to day… the king hearing complaints or petitions from others in the kingdom or may be having a party or he may be wanting to discuss issues with the nobles. Essentially, the courtroom of the king is where all the important people dwelled. It was the "happenin" place where you got to see and talk to the king often. Seeing the king frequently was especially important in times past, because the king was not easily seen by, or accessible to, the common people. The noble men and women on the other hand, had access to talk to the king and discuss the course of the nation, to support the king in his agenda, using their resources to see the king's will be done. In many ways, the true power of a king laid in the strength of his courtroom, because the nobles in the court would be the true ones to see the king's justice go forth.

The king entrusted his nobles to manage his kingdom in ways that pleased and reflected him. If a noble upset the king, he could be dismissed from the court, essentially put in a timeout and not allowed to come to the palace. This was a painful punishment carrying shame and dishonor. But when the king's disapproval past, he could invite that same noble back and replace the shame with honor.

So we are the Church—The Ecclesia— and when we gather, it is not an event or program or glorified concert but a royal people flowing with the heart of the King that day. We are to be experiencing court. We come to Him as noble people, rulers of the earth and we show up together to adore and worship Him, to hear from Him and also petition Him on behalf of the earth. We may even make decrees connected to His heart. See, what we typically call church, is actually a courtroom. And we brothers and sisters, we are His noblemen. His princes and princesses.

Holding Court

Court is inherently exciting. Not just because of music or who is speaking that day, but because of the wonder of what is on the heart of the King. As we gather, we access His voice, excited to be partnering with Him and His will. When we come together as an earthly courtroom, we connect with the heavenly courtroom. We begin to mirror what is going on up there and administer His will through prayer and works of service. The courtroom is where the power is released as we pray for our neighborhoods, our nation and other nations.

> …when we gather, it is not an event or program or glorified concert but a royal people flowing with the heart of the King that day…We come to Him as noble people, rulers of the earth and we show up together to adore and worship Him…

Court is where we encourage one another and build one another up in the Lord. Court is a place where we move among other nobles and learn from each other. How do we love one another? How do we rule more effectively in our spheres of influence? We must begin to identify ourselves as a court and walk as a powerful group of people who can determine the fate of a nation. We must fight to have unity under our King—domain with the other nobles. A courtroom spells trouble for a king when the noblemen begin to fight with each other. Why? Such behavior weakens the king's causes—in earthly senses, it could even threaten his reign. Any good king would make it his duty to see there is unity amongst his courtroom of leaders, for the sake of his throne. We must see one another as individuals who are powerful: given access to the King and with authority from Him. As we come together unified under our King, we become an unstoppable force, we become the feared Ecclesia that the gates of hell cannot stop.

Tell them to "Follow you"

Up until this point, we have covered that the kingdom of God is not a figurative kingdom, but a real one. That we as individual believers are royalty and make up the noble court of our King. We have been seated on thrones as His children. As children of God, we have been given the highest titles in the Kingdom: beloved heirs. Together, as children—heirs and heiresses—we are His court of nobles, powerful ones under His leadership, sworn to serve His house.

One day, I was in my kitchen when the Lord brought to mind the Scripture, when Paul says "….that each of you says, 'I am of Paul,' or 'I am of Apollos,' or 'I am of Cephas,' or 'I am of Christ.' Is Christ divided" (1 Corinthians 1:12)? Then I heard God say, "When you all normally speak on that verse you are making the point that there is no division in me— and that's good. But, did you ever consider that there was nothing inherently wrong in them identifying as "of Paul" and "of Silas"? I stopped in my tracks as I caught up with the weight of this consideration. Right after hearing that, I saw a picture in my head of Jesus walking on the beach telling his future disciples to follow Him. And then I heard God say, "Start to tell people to follow you."

At the time when Jesus called out to his prospective disciples, He was just thirty years old. I was thirty-two when God spoke like this to me in my kitchen. Pondering it all, this question came to my mind, *What caused the disciples to leave everything and follow you, Jesus?* They didn't know He was God, not right away, not until the Spirit would reveal it. Why would they leave their livelihood and follow this stranger? And then it occurred to me. They had a kingdom mindset. When the disciples first saw Yeshua, He walked and talked like a man of importance. Royalty. They didn't hesitate to follow Him because they didn't want to miss out on the opportunity to have the honor of being connected to Him. They wanted to be more than just common men.

Paul spoke in this same pattern. He made a call with an inherent expectation that others would follow. He said, "Follow me as I follow Christ" (1 Corinthians 11:1). How were there so many references to people identifying themselves with certain apostles or households? Because of this very pattern of a call to discipleship. This looks very different than our reality in the West. We have an individual mindset. We do our best to set each person on a "personal relationship with God". We tell them to read the Bible or to go to church meetings on Sunday, but we never say "follow me." Jesus said it. And so, Paul followed suit: "follow me as I follow Christ." Just as when we translate our knowledge of royalty into royal language, we run the risk of being seen as proud or weird—that is the risk here. But really, it is an arrogant, selfish thing not to tell people to follow you. We leave new babies in the Lord to navigate the jungle of the world and make it to the other side. Many do, by God's grace, but I'm sure we all are aware that many don't make it and leave the faith.

Having a leader with God's heart is a blessing and a gift. Being a leader with God's heart is a mutual blessing and a gift. Like with kingdom language, both the receiver and giver are beneficiaries. When we humble ourselves, God can use such a leader to make another stronger and wiser in the things of the Spirit and assist in a person's predestined calling. Being kingdom-minded is in fact submitting to noble leadership, becoming like little children as Jesus commanded.

Following like a Child

Could this be why God said, the key to the kingdom is becoming like a little child? Jesus said in Mark 10:9, "Truly I say to you whoever does not receive the kingdom of God as a little child will by no means enter it." Whoa. We better get this right then. Many points hang on this teaching. Namely, in order to come to faith in Jesus, there is a point where logic stops and simple belief starts; Just as a child believes what they're told just because you told them. This is not to make less of research and fact collecting, which point us to Jesus as the Messiah. But it is to say, at the end of your study and research you still have to believe that a God-man was raised up from the grave, ascended into heaven and will come back riding on the clouds! This belief is a miraculous work of the Spirit, that can only take root in a childlike heart.

Being childlike bleeds into how we operate with each other. Jesus would listen to the disciples go on and on with each other about who would be greater in the Kingdom. We must remember that their Master ushered them in with the call of the kingdom. John the Baptist proclaimed across the land that Jesus was the very fulfillment of the kingdom being at-hand (Matthew 3:1).

The disciples' argument, at least the context, makes sense. I believe that Jesus wanted them to think on the kingdom more. I believe Jesus delighted in them envisioning the kingdom and aspiring to top leadership there. I believe Jesus liked the fact that they wanted to be great. The problem in the disciples' argument was not the desire to be great in the kingdom, but their dim, human way of aspiring to it.

> The problem in the disciples' argument was not the desire to be great in the kingdom, but their dim, human way of aspiring to it.

When Jesus saw the children playing around his disciple huddle, He saw a great opportunity for teaching. He called the little child to Himself. In my imagination, the toddling child came right away and sat on his lap and waited until the grown-up was done talking about something and released her or him to go back to play. The child had no pride. The child Jesus called had nothing to be prideful of. He or she did not care about how she was being viewed. When little children meet one another, they do not size each other up based on status and accomplishments, they simply want to play and be silly. The child on Jesus' lap is unaware that God Himself is declaring to humanity, *you must be converted to become like this very little child*.

To Be Great, We Must Serve

To even begin to become great we have to become like little children who do not fight over titles and positions. We accept the role we have been given and walk in it with joy. Why? Because we love and trust the giver of our role. We should not be compared to the next one. We must become like a child, listening to one another with respect. We must become those disinterested with the praises of men and contented with the truth that we belong to our Father.

Everything we have is because of God. Our very existence is because of His good will. The reason we are in the kingdom at all, is because Jesus paved the way. And the reason we have any role in the eternal kingdom is because it brings the Father joy. So let us trust the fact that God wants us to have the highest position in heaven. As the Ecclesia, we are His highest, noble elect, and only He decides the roles within that call here on earth and in heaven. Let us trust His leadership to get us fully into the role, not by manipulation or fighting among ourselves. No, on the contrary, the very way to attain our high calling is to serve one another. Jesus says,

Whoever receives one of these little children like this in my name receives me. And whoso shall receive one such little child in my name receives me. (Matthew 18:5)

Jesus makes it clear that we should be walking in childlikeness and we should be receiving each other in this way. The wise reversal here is that the world's standard of greatness is walking in pride of your accomplishments and only respecting those who have accomplished greatness. In God's kingdom, we actually should, "do nothing from selfish ambition or conceit, but in humility count others more significant than yourselves" (Philippians 2:3). We are not to assign ourselves any more importance beyond our given royal status—heir and child of the highest royal family in the earth and heavens. We are unassuming, and yet very much a confident child.

Jesus says, "…whoever receives one little child like this in my name receives me" (Matthew 18:5). It is all the more important then, never to take childlike faith and stature lightly, because in doing so, we take King Jesus lightly.

> It is all the more important then, never to take childlike faith and stature lightly, because in doing so, we take King Jesus lightly.

Do you want to receive Jesus when he shows up? I want to receive Jesus! He might not show up looking like a very distinguished royal, instead He may appear a lighthearted royal child. Are you a little one? In order to really see the kingdom of God come to earth as it is in heaven, being converted to become like a little child is a must.

Arya Stark is part of the royal family of Stark but doesn't let that stop her from being a tomboy getting dirty and not looking like a "lady". I love the scene when she is trying to get back to the court yard and the palace guards think she is some street girl. They say something to the effect of, "off with you no begging" and they threaten her with a smack on the rear. To that she responds, " I'm Arya Stark of Winterfell. If you lay a hand on me my father will have both your heads on spikes. Now, are you going to let me by or do I need to smack you on the ears to help you with your hearing." Arya Stark knows who she is and who her father is. She is not shy about letting them know the power she has through her father. Connection: We are God's children no matter if people perceive it as such or not. We should know that we belong in the palace of God and shouldn't let anyone talk us out of that. In confidence, we let anyone who stands in our way know the punishment that will take place if they lay a hand on us. Arya is a princess so move out of her way. Likewise, we are royal children, so gates of hell move out of the way!

Chapter Three

Kingdom Government Part 1: The Family

We serve the triune, great, King—Alpha and Omega. We serve Him as little children, taking Him at His Word, while not taking ourselves too seriously. Treating the brethren as worthy of loyalty and respect, in honor of our share in the household of saints. All of this is foundational to establishing a kingdom government. Now, we must talk about how all of this is walked out in a real tangible way. How is this organized for the glory of the Lord?

> And the government will be upon His shoulder. And His name will be called Wonderful, Counselor, Mighty God, Everlasting Father, Prince of Peace. Of the increase of His government and peace there will be no end. (Isaiah 9:6)

God's kingdom is a government, an order from the smallest position to the highest. In order for it to function right (namely that His kingdom will be on the earth as it is in heaven) I propose that the Ecclesia, the Church, should be organized in the way that every kingdom has been—a family tree. And through these families—a house model. The ruling Ecclesia should operate like a real royal family, made up of many smaller, organized royal families, called "Houses" (See Appendix A).

The following order could not be possible without first settling who we are as sons and daughters of King Jesus and how we are to see other sons and daughters, in the Spirit. Hence, chapters one and two. When this is not in place, pride will set in and we will compete against each other, in our own service to God. Instead, we must celebrate one another's accomplishments and positions in His kingdom from a heart of thanks.

Family

One day I heard the Lord say to me, "It's all about family." What a simple truth that I thought I knew. The Lord revealed to me how much I did not get this. For years I had done ministry and my wife supported me in it. When the Lord spoke to me, I realized I wasn't ministering to her. I immediately went on a mission to minister to my wife consistently, and with her—to be her support and partner. The Lord wasn't stopping there. As my wife and I began ministering together, the Lord directed me to start "building my house." To begin to call people to "follow me" and to join our spiritual family in Christ, and our physical family. Essentially, I took His call to mean, "Follow me as I follow Christ." I crafted a family motto, mission, and we invited those who need/ed a spiritual family to join under our covering. This was with the intent to partner with other houses called to do the same thing.

Building a House

I was fueled by God's example in ancient Israel. When setting up the kingdom of Israel, He did it through the household of Jacob (also known as Israel), the descendent of Abraham, of whom God made his promise to bless the nations (Genesis 12:1-3). From Jacob's household came twelve sons, and each of those sons seeded a tribe, creating the twelve tribes of Israel. Each tribe was known for specific identities in gifts, talents and roles within the nation. It seems clear that the twelve different tribes were broken up into families, from great ones to small ones. One famous story that clearly illustrates this is in 1 Samuel 9:21, when God calls Saul to become king of Israel. Saul says to the prophet Samuel, "am I not a Benjamint of the smallest of the tribes of Israel and my family the least of all the families of The Tribe of Benjamin?"

Similarly, I believe that the house model is what the Lord is calling the Ecclesia to enter into. In some ways, we have been walking in this model by the Spirit already. In the West, we start a church and we think of a name for the church. We brand it with a logo. And if we are honest, these churches are built on the personality of the founder or leader. Yes, we may like the music and other aspects, but we mostly have to decide if we trust and like the head Pastor. *Is this someone I can listen to week after week, instructing me on the ways of life and godliness?* The head pastor of the local church is in many ways, vital to whether the church lives or dies. Often, if a church has a split, it breaks between two different pastors and people normally pick sides based on who they trust and declare their loyalty. Churches have formal names, but essentially, they are "The house of [insert leader]". This is how I believe heaven sees them. We call these leaders shepherds, and if they are in fact shepherds, then we are sheep.

In the evangelical world, many people may say this is not a good thing. *Our attendance should not be based on a human leader.* At one point in my walk, I would have agreed with this notion. But when God began unveiling this kingdom model to me, I began to realize that the leadership under which we submit is key. Let's be very clear: Every church should ultimately submit to one leader— and that is Jesus himself. He is the head of all families, households and churches. King Jesus rules over them in love, compassion, mercy and justice. He is the cornerstone on which we build our house (Psalm 118:22) But there is a pervasive hierarchy that we see unfold under this ultimate headship. This is no new idea. Houses making up God's chosen kingdom is biblical, from the First Testament to the Second:

The Lord grant mercy to the household of Onesiphorus, for he often refreshed me, and was not ashamed of my chain; (2 Timothy 1:16)

All the saints greet you, but especially those who are of Caesar's household. (Philippians 4:22)

Yes, I also baptized the household of Stephanas. Besides, I do not know whether I baptized any other. (1 Corinthians 1:16)

For it has been declared to me concerning you, my brethren, by those of Chloe's *household,* that there are contentions among you. (1 Corinthians 1:11)

Greet Herodion, my countryman. Greet those who are of the *household* of Narcissus who are in the Lord. (Romans 16:11)

Then Crispus, the ruler of the synagogue, believed on the Lord with all his household. And many of the Corinthians, hearing, believed and were baptized. (Acts 18:8)

So they said, "Believe on the Lord Jesus Christ, and you will be saved, you and your household." (Acts 16:31)

"Who then is a faithful and wise servant,
whom his master made ruler over his household,
to give them food in due season?" (Matthew
24:45)

The Bible assumes that the Church is broken up by households. This is evident all throughout the apostles' letters. Jesus told John in the book of Revelation, to address his letter to the Angel of Sardis, Laodiceans, Smyrna and others (Rev 2/3). Who are these people? They are the head leaders of the Ecclesia in that city! And under them are faithful households, of which they oversee. Do you see now, how the kingdom of God was always meant to be a kingdom, even on this earth, and established in order? Since we are a kingdom, the current model many churches choose to operate in—a corporation or business—is not the full picture.

Regent Leadership

Imagine with me. If a King of a nation leaves for a time, he puts a "regent" in charge. That regent operates in the King's absence as interim king. The people are supposed to treat him as such. I believe this is how every pastor over a church should view themselves— interim kings of the Most High God. In other words, a physical stand-in for Jesus. What is a shepherd to a sheep anyway? He is King over the sheep.

Now the reason we call pastors "shepherds", is to highlight the way they should lead: tenderly, loving the body of believers and caring for them. The shepherd is a humble position of leadership and the sheep know their shepherd's voice. Without a shepherd, the sheep will get lost and die.

A shepherd attempts to heal the sheep. He keeps them trimmed, healthy and protected. Likewise, this is the role of a king over his dominion. Jesus is the Great Shepherd (Hebrews 13:20). He is the King of glory, who reigns over heaven and earth. Because of this, when men take the role of shepherd in His physical absence, really, they are taking on the role of regent, or interim king. Anyone who wants to recognize a man as their pastor, is essentially recognizing him as a regent ruler, sent by the Lord to oversee them and lead them in the way the King of kings would want.

I understand that this is hard to agree with in the United States of America. We are rooted in the notion of rejecting a kingdom and a democratic republic. But let us not forget, God is not asking for our opinion! His rule is already happening in heaven and will soon come to earth. All the nations will bow to Him and every place will be under the King who reigns from Mount Zion in Israel (Isaiah 23:23). The kingdom of God is here, because it's within us (Luke 17:20-21). His people coming out, to be seen by all, is only right of the Ecclesia. Haven't we established that we are the ruling body? We are to begin to not only walk in its character and holiness, but also as an organized Kingdom.

> See this. Every church is a portion of territory in the Kingdom of God.

See this. Every church is a portion of territory in the Kingdom of God. Since the King of kings is in heaven, He has put shepherds (regents) in place to lead His church (noble court meeting in a house) in His absence. In every church (noble court meeting in a house), there are kings (heads of households), by nature of our royal status as Christians. These kings join and submit to the headship (regent) who is overseeing a specific part of the greater kingdom's vision. These kings (heads of households) have their own vision and a mission, and they submit in service to other households for the sake of strengthening the regent's overarching vision. When this is done right, it will be a beautiful picture of heavenly greatness for the Lord. Jesus said in Matthew 20:25,

> But Jesus called them to Himself and said, 'You know that the rulers of the Gentiles lord it over them, and those who are great exercise authority over them. Yet it shall not be so among you; but whoever desires to become great among you, let him be your servant. And whoever desires to be first among you, let him be your slave— just as the Son of Man did not come to be served, but to serve, and to give His life a ransom for many.'

Wow. Here is Christian culture. Can we truly live like this? We have so much focus on our own individual callings, that we rarely think to become someone else's slave, or submit ourselves to another's vision, in order to reach our calling and dreams. Yet, the Kingdom of God is exactly this. It looks like submitting our lives to one another, fully concerned about those who we are serving, and them reaching their calling; Together, trusting that God will see to it that our calling will not be forgotten, but in fact secure it coming to fruition, when He sees fit.

Remember Jesus in Matthew 20:26? In short, if you want to become great, become someone else's servant. This is amazing! Instead of fighting to become great, we should be fighting to become one another's slave, so we will be great in heaven.

> …if you want to become great, become someone else's servant.

Imagine these young men, the disciples. They are trying to solidify their eternal position by stating how gifted and talented they are. Jesus flips the script entirely. Based on His direction, the disciples are going around the room saying, "Okay. I will be your slave" and the next the same "I will be your slave" …and the one who finds himself in-charge of the twelve, is now scrambling to find someone to serve. Do you see what God has done? A race to the bottom to get to the top. I know we feel called to serve people groups sometimes. But I believe Jesus wanted us to actually find an individual to become a royal servant to.

Moving forward, I will begin to talk about how the kingdom house model serves this end of service to one another. I will provide specific examples of how the model functions, and why, as we get closer to the end of the age and the return of Jesus, the house model is necessary.

Kings

Every house should be run like a kingdom model, with a king as head of the home. A kings qualifications are like that of the elder in the book of (1 Timothy 3:1-7). An of age male who has captured what it means to be a godly leader and father. The foundation of any house is the most important, this foundation is the role of the king, or head of household.

The survival of the house is dependent on the heart, wisdom and leadership of the king in the house. Is this man a man of prayer, humility, strength and vision? The head of house should be a fervent prayer warrior, righteous in character. If so, he can lead his house to the moon and back, safely—while taking on new territory that has never been taken. James says that if you,

> Confess *your* trespasses to one another, and pray for one another, that you may be healed. The effective, fervent prayer of a righteous man avails much. (James 5:16)

Men have a special gift, and that is the gift of vision. Providing vision (foresight or plan) to a goal is what men do best. Men have a unique gift of building things. I believe, when men look at a problem they can begin to see how to build it or fix it. We are the ones who are supposed to lay out a vision for ourselves and families, clarifying where we are going and why. Men cast vision

47

of purpose and calling. We set a course and put the family in their place to reach the destination, or destiny.

Men also have a gift in the area of protection. One only has to look at any nation's military and see that men most often volunteer to join the military, and vow to protect the nation even if it comes to laying down their own lives. Men have it in them to protect friends and family; they are rightfully willing to prevent harm coming to their loved ones. Men's sense of protection is especially important when it comes to leading a house. Men are looking out for what could harm their house, this includes: lies, oppression and deception. A godly man will fight like a pro-boxer to see these things rooted out of the family.

Men are an instrumental part of the house. I had a dream once, and in it, the Lord asked me, "Do you want wisdom?" I said, "Yes." And he said, "You will either be "the way" or the "insulation." I woke up. The "way" speaks to vision. I am to help people know the right way to go in life, in light of Jesus' soon return. The "insulation" speaks to keeping the cold winds of life outside, where a family is inside keeping warm. Men are designed to cover in these ways. Women do play a role in giving vision and protection, as I point out shortly. Men walk in these matters naturally and with more intensity. I believe, if there are women shepherds, they should be submitted and under the covering of a godly man, just like every male pastor should be in service to another male's house and his authority. This is in step with Scripture,

But I want you to realize that the head of
every man is Christ, and the head of the woman
is man, and the head of Christ is God. (1
Corinthians 11:3)

Men naturally take leadership from other men, and
the vision and covering of that male leader will bring
another dimension of who God is to that congregation
and his will. A godly, head of the house can play a
father figure role, brother, son, and use his natural gifts
and authority to help lead everyone to the right direction
internally and outwardly.

The head of a household, or king, should be into his
thirties and I do believe this leader should begin to
consider stepping down as head of the house when his
spiritual sons become in their thirties this is not a rule
but a suggestion because passing the torch is important
for any family to see growth from one generation to the
next. The victories of the aged fathers should inspire
the young to rise to overcome and fight ills of their
generation.

Queens

Every man who is leading in a house should be
married to a mighty woman of God. This is foundational
to a healthy house that is producing fruit. They make
disciples much in part, to her confidence in the regal
role that God has given her.

The wise woman builds her house, But the foolish pulls it down with her hands. (Proverbs 14:1)

Just as men have a unique calling and gifting, women also do. This is absolutely essential when it comes to running a healthy growing house. Like men, women are protectors, but in a different sense. Her male counterpart, the king, is called to serve and protect his queen and the whole house. Queens on the other hand, have the gift and calling to protect their king. Just like in the game of chess, the queen has the greatest amount of authority on the chessboard because her main objective is to protect the king.

A king may have the role to protect the nation, but the queen has the most important role— to protect the king. When a woman is confident that her king (rather it be her father, brother, son or a husband) is protecting her and all the people she loves, if she is mature and wise, she will indeed protect him in return. When the Bible says,

Likewise, husbands, live with your wives in an understanding way, showing honor to the woman as the weaker vessel, since they are heirs with you of the grace of life, so that your prayers may not be hindered. (1 Peter 3:7)

I am only saying what the Bible makes clear. The language here is so expressive of the point. The woman may be the weaker vessel, but she is honorable and a co-heir in the kingdom. So much so, that God says, He will not hear the fervent prayers of her king if he does not understand and honor her.

Additionally, let's consider the phrase "weaker vessel". When I reflect on that verse, I think of Superman and Wonder Woman. Anyone who knows anything about DC characters, specifically Superman and Wonder Woman, they would never say Wonder Woman is weak. If you are not on her side, this Amazon princess is a warrior and is to be feared. She is one of the major founders of the Justice League and her heroic reputation precedes her. The 2016 movie *Wonder Woman*, displayed her strength around the world. Her face, costume and might were heralded.

Nonetheless, no one would ever dare to say Wonder Woman is stronger than Superman. I have yet to see that debate. This is because, compared to Superman, Wonder Woman is the weaker vessel. Not because she is weak, but simply because there is another stronger. In this same way, the queen of a house holds an extremely powerful position. She will help keep the largest house in order. With her God-given talents, she will bring the king encouragement, exaltation, correction, and provision. The implications of this spill over into the entire house.

The Bible makes it clear that the role of wife was always meant to be a helper, a companion (Genesis 2:18) I believe her husband—king—may have the vision where things need to go, but the wife, the queen, has the gifting to see the details of that vision come forth. Women carry a gifting in planning and seeing details through. A queen's role is essential to see her king's vision unfold.

So, in building a strong house, a strong man of God and a strong woman of God in covenant with each other and agreement on the house's vision and mission, should be the foundation of a house. With their leadership reflecting the image of Jesus and His bride, the limits of the things they can accomplish have no bounds.

Princes, Princesses, Lords and Ladies

The house is built on the strength of the king and queen, but there are other roles to a strong royal family. An unmarried man is a prince or lord, likewise the unmarried woman is a princess or lady. When these men and women join a house, or are birthed in, they should be immediately addressed by their new royal names, as exhausted in chapter one. When we honor each other in our words by speaking our royal titles to each other, it builds everyone up.

In House Rush, we refer to them as prince or princess until they get married and start their own house and step into the role as king and queen. Since a house can only have one king or queen, the titles for the others are prince and princess, even though their destinies may very well be to one day step into king and queen of their own house. Prince or princess, is no childish title. Royal rights come with these names. They are well-respected and should be honored. Prince and princesses can be snot-nosed children or serious mini-kings and mini-queens, the difference is dependent upon their age and maturity. The princes and princesses should see the king and queen of the house as their spiritual father and mother (there are cases where they could be seen as natural parents as well) and give honor in word and action as such. A prince or princess of a house should partner with their spiritual parents to see the kingdom of God increase.

Any male adult who may be older or the same age as the king who may not be in a position spiritually as a son should be considered a "lord". Likewise, an adult female should be considered as a "lady". These are honored roles in a house where they have as much commitment to the leadership and vision as the children of a house should, but they take more of a brother/sister role.

When you have a culture of honor in your house, the way you address each other bleeds into many other areas of conduct. The way you disagree on things changes. The way you have patience with one another changes. The way you support each other begins to change. When you know you're dealing with a royal—and not just any royal, but royalty of heaven—you walk in a careful manner. Think on this deep sense of belonging. I have seen it so immensely powerful in House Rush. Ryan joins my house. He immediately becomes, "Prince Ryan of House Rush" in service to the King of Glory. This is who he is, now.

Every sheep needs a herd. I want to make clear that Jesus is the ultimate Shepherd. He is the source of life and in Him we lack nothing. The king and queen of a house do not play the role of "source of life". Every individual should be in a vibrant, personal relationship with God and should be hearing from Him directly and following His leadership. The house is a place of community, where God can speak to us through different relationships as family. God made us to be in community! His desire is to speak to you, encourage you and sustain you, through the other. Even still, please know, that if you were on an island, by yourself, God would provide all you needed in the Holy Spirit that dwells inside of you. He would not leave you or forsake you. He would commune with you there.

Small Council

Every house should have small council meetings. These are regularly scheduled, and attended by the king and queen of the house, the most loyal house member (seen as the third in command) and the king of another house that is in service to them (preferably the house most committed to them). A small counsel shouldn't be more than seven persons, and a minimum of three. They should meet to talk about the details of the house's business and planning. This is in addition to holding court and other house activities during the week.

Game of Thrones is based on a kingdom in Westeros. Westeros is broken up into seven different kingdoms. These kingdoms are distinguished by seven different families leading them. Under these families, you see smaller houses that are made up of individuals who pledge to serve them. Within the seven seasons of this show you see these houses interact in ways that are very entertaining—betrayal and honor to name a couple. One of the reasons the show is so loved, is how engrossing it is to begin rooting for a certain house. Watchers love to see the display of loyalty, even unto death. This interconnectedness of households, and unique roles of each house reflects the kingdom house model in many ways.

Chapter Four

Kingdom Government Part 2: House Administration

For years there has been ongoing debate on how church should be done. Many maintain the position that a house church (a church that meets in someone's home) is the best model. A group of people who meet in a house where they can be in close relationship built between people and where you can feel less as a number. Others say, that to reach more people, you pack as many as can fit into one big church to cultivate more energy and then create break-out discipleship models. Or, there is the mega-church and its many forms (multi-site/satellite) who rely on small groups, so individuals don't have to feel just like a face in the crowd. In my mind, it is not the mega-church model versus the house church. It is both. The royal family and families who meet under that family's covering, is a house church. But the network of houses in service to one another can be as large as a mega-church when convened. Let's discuss this in more detail.

Joining a House

You cannot feel like a number in this model, because of the order in which a household runs. Once you join you are immediately connected to the head of the house and his wife (king and queen)—you become their responsibility. The king should be praying for you, getting to know you, making sure your needs are being met and introducing you to the rest of the house. You become part of that house's royal family.

A house should have a regular set time where they all come together to worship, eat and have court (house church). Then, your household attends a convening weekly service made up of other households who are in-service to one another in varying capacities (could imply a mega-church). So, not only do you get the smaller, more intimate feeling of a community, but you also get connected to a larger piece of God's Kingdom. As you move among the larger gathering, even as a new person, you are operating from a place of acceptance because of the household in which you identify.

What is a sheep without a herd? What is a herd without a shepherd? Everyone has a need to be part of a family with a sense of belonging. When you are part of a household, you get that sense of family even if you are in a room of 10,000 people. Imagine with me, that you are a single person who shows up to a large convening of house churches—imagine it feels like a mega-church. You go, and you like it. You are thinking about joining a particular house, so you inquire. You are handed a long list of the meeting households, with their particular visions and contact info for the head of household. You sift through and narrow down visions that resonate with you. You meet with heads of established households—kings and queens—and hear with more clarity their mission statement, who they are and the culture of their court gatherings. You then gather all your data points, go into your prayer closet and make a decision on which house you want to join.

The process of choosing a house to join should be done walking in prayer and true understanding of the mission and goal of that household. There must be mutual agreement on the fit, between the new member and the head of household. Upon joining, you are afforded the entitlements of being family, with the expectation and charge, that you come ready to serve.

You are expected to submit yourself to the leadership of that house in the way of following them as they follow Christ. To listen to the heads of households and allow them to speak into your life. Allow the leadership of the house to shepherd you and cover you in the right way. You are expected to serve the house in accomplishing the mission the house has already laid out. You are expected to represent the house in the best way everywhere you go: in excellence, character and holiness.

A person who is part of a house should expect from the leader's guidance, a sense of protection and a level of attentiveness. The leadership should be providing for them space and opportunity to grow and to serve in their gifting. All this, again, can only be done with a humble heart from all parties. This is the kingdom of God and we must have some sort of biblical character of love and service to do things right. This is a summary of expectations of being part of a house which is different than being in service to a house.

Expanding a House

I do believe that every godly marriage is a house. Only after several years of walking together in marriage, and with a blessing from the house you serve, should your house begin to grow into a large/r one. Every married couple should be seeking to make disciples of others in so much as they have a healthy marriage. A very newly wedded couple should focus on loving each other and growing in maturity with each other. There comes a time though, where they can be a force for good together as they disciple and invite others to join their family. I believe this couple should be in service to another house where they see it done and learn from the heart of servant kings and queens.

When that time comes, a couple serving another house shouldn't have any trouble receiving a blessing from that house as they begin to grow their house and welcome families in. The purpose of marriage is to shine the light and to reflect the mystery of Jesus and His bride. There is so much power in the love that permeates a godly couple. Leaning on each other's gifts and collective strength of commitment to each other is godly. The power released, when a man and woman anointed by God agree on a matter, cannot be measured! This is why I believe a single man or woman can serve for mighty purposes within a household but would be insufficient in leading a house on their own.

> The power released, when a man and woman anointed by God agree on a matter, cannot be measured!

Every house should attempt to have a motto, mission, family Psalm, along with a small description of who they are. That description should include what houses they're in service to. This upfront work, creates a deep identity for the members of the house and will call them higher. The house motto and mission, ladders up to the whole body of Christ's mission. In 1 Corinthians 12, Paul discusses the multi-faceted nature of the body of Christ. We should operate in this way. Realizing we are one whole, made up of different parts, with different functions, the members of a house, but still one body.

Being In Service to a House

Every house has their own identity: their own mission. It doesn't need to be totally different from every other house but the distinctions should include motto and signet (or tagline and logo). When a house is in service to another house, it dedicates their house margin to assisting the mission of that house, to help them reach the fullness of their calling. A household that is being served by another is not overseeing everything that house does. Instead, you take on a serving posture. There remains mutual respect for the other house's leadership and there is trust and honor between them.

A house in service to another is expected to follow the broad leadership of the house, be under accountability of that house and be looking for ways to help that house grow in strength. They are pledged to serve to the best of their ability, in the grace of God, with the greatest amount of loyalty and pledge to arise when called. A house that is being served is expected to give that house certain levels of authority. Allow the most faithful of that house's leadership to sit at its small council, give that house respect and honor and lead them courageously.

The individuals in a house should be in service to the house and actually participate in helping the mission of the house come to fulfillment. Every house should also be in service to another house to see the same thing manifest.

I want to illustrate this type of service for you. A dear friend shared a vision with me, that God gave him. I found God speaking to me about my spiritual brother's large vision and I soon had a notebook full of details to make his vision a reality and run well. After some time of sharing my many thoughts and excitement with him, I started to wonder if I should really lead it altogether; I knew he didn't have a lot of details down. As I was thinking about this, I hear the Lord say to me, "Why don't you let him lead it and serve him the way you will want people to serve you in the vision I give you." Whoa. It didn't take long to see the genius of God at work. The Lord was calling my house, House Rush, to submit and to serve another king's house, House Williams. The Lord was calling me to trust God with his destiny and to trust that there would be no forfeit of my own in giving of my margin and time. House William's destiny was not at odds with mine, because we are of the same Kingdom. By serving another's house, we ensure that the kingdom does not become divided.

God may call you to humble yourself and recognize a leader by the Spirit, versus impressive presentation. This means He might call you to a king or queen that are unlikely candidates for leaders in the world's eyes. This may mean following someone who seems "green". But doing so, allows the forming of an army that is unified, strong, humble and in order. There are reasons we may need to follow different kings; namely, there are so many different facets to expanding God's kingdom on the earth.

We know only One is worthy to lead the Church at large. There is only One, King of kings, who is worthy to be followed. But this King, calls us to follow the Christ-like example of one another.

In western Christian culture, we sometimes obsess over "callings". We forget that we are actually called to serve someone else's calling. I am convinced that every house should be in service to another to be connected to a vision even bigger than their own. In this way, so much humility is brought to the table. No matter how big a house gets, it is still in service to another. In this way, we limit division within the body by exposing its interconnectedness. The king and queen of the house still bend their knee to another king and queen. A house cannot be an island to itself when it is submitted to another. The house the Lord calls you to, should be led by a man who loves the Lord with all his heart. Who has been tested and found true over a period of time. Someone who is not led by their personal emotions or fear of man. Someone who has a clear track record of holiness and vision for his house and follows the lamb wherever he goes. A man worthy of following is not a perfect one, but one who follows the perfect One. Like Paul said, "Follow me as I follow Christ." The family within a house yields to the king. Not because they agree with him all of the time but because they trust he has their best interest in mind and the king has no problem admitting when he is wrong.

> A man worthy of following is not a perfect one, but one who follows the perfect One.

God may not call you to serve someone who is smarter than you or wiser in the earthly sense. He may call you to serve someone who is younger, less educated or talk with an accent you struggle hearing. Many love to serve the head pastor of a megachurch in hopes one day they will have their moment of promotion and recognition…but how many of the same people are willing to serve a house or pastor that has little to offer in the way of promotion before the eyes a man?

Whoever the Lord calls you to serve, do so fully. This is a wise choice. You will be surprised how God will make it all count in eternity and how the fruit shows up on the earth. You may be smarter, wiser and more mature then the whole house He calls you to be in service to, but that might be the exact reason He called you there—so you can use those talents as offerings to help another who may be in need. Submitting in this way is heavenly humility.

Financial Service

I never will forget when the Lord said to me, "Chris, what about the money?" I was like, "What about the money?" God then began to show me how money can flow and flourish within this model. It begins with clear ministry expenses and committed tithing.

For example, House Jones is a small house and they have $200 of ministry expenses that they spend a month, this includes: a weekly Bible study where they feed those that attend and provide Bibles to newcomers. Let's say that between Mr. and Mrs. Jones and one other noble who has joined their house, they have $500 worth of tithe money. House Jones should first cover their $200 ministry expenses, and then give the $300 difference to the house they are in service to; let's say that house is, House Smith.

House Smith is of course practicing the same system of giving. Let's say that house Smith has $1,000 worth of ministry expenses (again, money they use to expand the kingdom through their house). Their tithe total is roughly $3,000. So, House Smith covers their $1000 expenses first from the tithe, and take that remaining $2,000 and give that to the house they are in service to.

Because of the interconnectedness of house ministry, there should ideally be no financial want or need. This is a beautiful model because it creates a way that every house can have funds to do ministry and to be transparent to the house they are in service to. This can empower more to step into missional initiatives without the fear of financial dismay. This also helps when people are in need. They can first go to the king and queen of their house and together determine if it is a real need and if they can help that person financially. If the house can't afford to help them out of their abundance, then they can petition the house they are in service to, or a larger house that is a service to them, in attempt to cover that need. This model helps more people while protecting the abuse of funds because of the close transparency.

Let's refer back to House Smith. Princess Tiffany has just joined House Smith. She hopes to use this model for personal gain, so she petitions the house leaders to help cover her bills for a month. Upon joining House Smith she was required to disclose her financial status, debt, and income to the small council, making them privy to her degree of real need. Princess Tiffany could choose to lie greatly and claim an emergency, but that would be an unsustainable way to obtain funds from the house. It would become clear, sooner than later, that she was trying to take advantage.

This also works conversely. Let's say Princess Michelle joins the house and is faithfully contributing tithe. She gets into a bad car accident and can't work because of it. In that case, the house could supplement her living expenses until she recovers.

We see this model of collective care in the beginning of the church movement where people brought all their belongings to help everyone: "… and [they] sold their possessions and goods, and divided them among all, as anyone had need" (Acts 2:45). The apostles made sure all who had need were provided for. This house model makes for a royal family who not only meets the spiritual needs of individuals but also natural needs. The Lord says, "…Bring all the tithes into the storehouse, That there may be food in My house…" (Malachi 3:8-10). When God says this, He's desiring that the Ministers of God are provided for, so they can feed the people of God with His Word and that the people who are ultimately under the Lord's house are eating and being provided for. This works well among people who are dedicated to the apostles' teachings and a common lifestyle.

Now the multitude of those who believed were of one heart and one soul; neither did anyone say that any of the things he possessed was his own, but they had all things in common. And with great power the apostles gave witness to the resurrection of the Lord Jesus. And great grace was upon them all. (Acts 4:32-33)

Before we can do Acts 4:32, we must have all things in common. A house has to understand who they are and what prophetic hour they are living in. When you are in- service to another house (and, or part of one) this does not mean you lose who you are as an individual or your identity as a house. You still have gifting as an individual that makes you unique. You still have a calling and it is right to move in the direction of your destiny the Lord has for you in His timing. Do things that you feel need to be done, but in doing so, you continue to serve another to reach their destiny, this keeps us from falling in the ditch of becoming to "me" focused. You will be a greater person when you are making others great.

If you are a Game of Thrones fan you definitely love the scene in season one and seven, when the houses of the North pledge their loyalty to Robb Stark and then Jon Snow. A great sense of loyalty and service is displayed as tough men lead other grown tough men and pledge their service to one another. Even when the other is younger and may seem less wise, there is a conviction that the leadership call on the individual will move everyone to the next level— it's inspiring!

Chapter Five

Kingdom Government Part 3: Conflict & Concerns

Undoubtable, there will be problems in houses. People are people and until the New Jerusalem comes to the Earth, our imperfections will be part of what we have to work through until we get there. The house model should help us work through these problems more sufficiently. When a house sees and understands the leadership structure, personal and corporate problems can be worked out in an orderly and careful fashion.

I believe when the Church begins to recognize the expanse of God's kingdom, and the many ways in which we need to support one another for the Kingdom to touch all peoples, it will make a beautiful sound, and a sweet smelling fragrance. "Behold, how good and

how pleasant *it is* For brethren to dwell together in
unity" (Psalms 133:1).

Clear Hierarchy

Everyone in the house should know who is in
authority over them and who they have under their
authority and care, if any. When a problem shows up,
the king, queen, council and service network, should be
able—with guidance from the Holy Spirit—to figure it
out. If the initial leadership cannot sufficiently handle
the matter, then the next level leadership must be
sought. The Bible lays out how a problem should be
handled,

> Moreover if your brother sins against you, go
> and tell him his fault between you and him alone.
> If he hears you, you have gained your brother.
> But if he will not hear, take with you one or two
> more, that 'by the mouth of two or three
> witnesses every word may be established.' And
> if he refuses to hear them, tell *it* to the church.
> But if he refuses even to hear the church, let him
> be to you like a heathen and a tax collector.
> (Matthew 18:15-17)

When a house problem needs the attention of the
king and queen, they will address the situation and
bring resolve. This works because everyone is in
agreement of the imperfect, but divinely appointed
leadership structure. This structure should be
respected, honored and heeded.

But what if the problem lies with the king or queen of a house? First, we have to be sure the problem is in fact the leader, and not our willingness to submit to that leader.

When finding fault with a house king or queen, we must honestly pray and discern if our issue is with the king or queen straying from the King of kings Himself—or if the issue is in fact, our pride or fear, keeping us from submitting to them. Revisiting the qualifications for leadership of a household is helpful in discerning what camp we fall into.

With this said, it should go without saying, that if a person is in clear compromise of a teaching—meaning, practicing heresy, then the proper steps must be taken.

> Brothers, if anyone is caught in any transgression, you who are spiritual should restore him in a spirit of gentleness. Keep watch on yourself, lest you too be tempted. (Galatians 6:1)

In short, do not follow anyone to hell. We must watch carefully over ourselves.

> Who may ascend the mountain of the LORD? Who may stand in his holy place? The one who has clean hands and a pure heart, who does not trust in an idol or swear by a false god. Psalm 24:3-4

Then how should the problem be addressed? If an issue arises with the king of the house keeping with the biblical protocol, you should approach the king to air your grievances in accordance with Matthew 18:

> If your brother sins against you, go and tell him his fault, between you and him alone. If he listens to you, you have gained your brother. But if he does not listen, take one or two others along with you, that every charge may be established by the evidence of two or three witnesses. If he refuses to listen to them, tell it to the church. And if he refuses to listen even to the church, let him be to you as a Gentile and a tax collector. (Matthew 18:15-17)

If that is done and there is no solution to the grievance then I would appeal to his wife, the queen, to see if she is able to come up with a solution. If that fails, then you should begin what I call the 1-2-3 solution. Every house should have a leadership structure laid out. In the event that the king of the house (which you are in) is in a clear place of sin, you should go to the leader of the house to which your house is most loyal in service to: the number one house. Loyalty is determined by various factors, including: representation of that house on your house's small council, degree of intimacy cultivated between the houses' members, time spent together, and financial contributions.

Example. House A is experiencing strife between the king and a member of the royal family. House B, is the most loyal house to House A. Members of House A loop in the king of House B. If the king of House B agrees with your grievances, then he would approach House A and appeal a hearing ear and repentance if needed. House B, though loyal to House A, is not a lapdog house. They should be the most zealous house out of many that know intricately the destiny and desire of that house. Therefore, they are advocates for removing anything that hinders that destiny. The king of House B will stand with you for a godly solution. In the case that the king of House A, refuses the counsel of the king from House B, then now as allies (House A's member along with House B's king) should approach the two kings of the houses that are over House A. If the two kings that are over House A agree with the brought grievances, then they should approach House A's king and queen and resolve the issue clearly. House A is in service to another house and is in a position where they have to consider greatly the kings' words of these houses.

In what I consider a very rare situation, House A may refuse to repent of sin when approached by the two houses above them. The three houses addressing House A will need to make a royal judgement on how to move forward and clearly communicate that judgment to everyone in House A, including the queen, along with every house who is in service to House A. Finally, if House A is in major, unrepentant sin, then clear separation/excommunication needs to happen. The two kings above House A will have the responsibility to communicate to all kings of houses in service to House

A the detail of the unrepentant sin and the attempted restorative process/es.

Let's consider the scenario playing out differently. Let's say you are the one in House A with the grievance, and you bring it to your king and queen, and they do not agree with your grievance and make no plan for addressing it. You then bring the matter to the king and queen of House B. If that king doesn't agree with you, you all could consider approaching the house that is above House A and start the process for resolve there.

The aim of such royal protocol and process is decency and order. Paul speaks of this in 1 Corinthians,

> Dare any of you, having a matter against another, go to law before the unrighteous, and not before the saints? Do you not know that the saints will judge the world? And if the world will be judged by you, are you unworthy to judge the smallest matters? Do you not know that we shall judge angels? How much more, things that pertain to this life? If then you have judgments concerning things pertaining to this life, do you appoint those who are least esteemed by the church to judge? I say this to your shame. Is it so, that there is not a wise man among you, not even one, who will be able to judge between his brethren? But brother goes to law against brother, and that before unbelievers! (1 Corinthians 6:2-6)

Paul clearly saw the church, the Ecclesia, as organized to the extent that we shouldn't need man's court when we have major issues with fellow Christians. I see this model making that possible.

Cults vs. House

At first introduction, the kingdom of God model may look like a cult. A branch of Christianity gone astray or radical. It is for this reason that being clear on royal protocol is so important. The model is designed to ensure scriptural accountability and authority when there is any stray from biblical love and holiness. If done right from the start, there really is no space for cult like behavior. When small councils are in place and every house is in service to another, it makes for a sure protection that prolonged abuse and rogue behavior will not take place.

Let's talk about cults further. There's no doubt that there will be people who may think this model is cultish. We should share in our concern and objection to such things. The Bible is clear, this is the good guardedness of a Christian.

As a result, we are no longer to be children, tossed here and there by waves and carried about by every wind of doctrine, by the trickery of men, by craftiness in deceitful scheming (Ephesians 4:14)

This command I entrust to you, Timothy, my son, in accordance with the prophecies previously made concerning you, that by them you fight the good fight, keeping faith and a good conscience, which some have rejected and suffered shipwreck in regard to their faith. Among these are Hymenaeus and Alexander, whom I have handed over to Satan, so that they will be taught not to blaspheme (1 Timothy 1:18-20).

But avoid worldly and empty chatter, for it will lead to further ungodliness, and their talk will spread like gangrene. Among them are Hymenaeus and Philetus, men who have gone astray from the truth saying that the resurrection has already taken place, and they upset the faith of some. (2 Timothy 2:16-18)

For there are many rebellious men, empty talkers and deceivers, especially those of the circumcision, who must be silenced because they are upsetting whole families, teaching things they should not teach for the sake of sordid gain. (Titus 1:10-11)

Merriam-Webster (2019) outlines cults as:

: great devotion to a person, idea, object, movement, or work (such as a film or book)
        criticizing how the media promotes the cult of
        celebrity
    ; especially : such devotion regarded as a literary or intellectual fad

: the object of such devotion

c : a usually small group of people characterized by such devotion

the singer's cult of fans (Webster dictionary, 2019)

If the above definition is embraced, then the film industry is a cult. Sports fanatics can form cults. Gamers have cults. Cults by this definition are all around us in the form of an obsession by a group of people regarding a person or idea. Game of Thrones has created cult-like behavior around the world! Of course, we typically don't think of the secular obsessions as being part of a cult, we immediately go to religion. Even as Christians, we do this and for good reason. We think of existing cults that operate exclusive to the world and put all their hope and independence into a leader and it ends terribly. We think of people like Jim Jones, and we project the fear of a do-over onto new initiatives and ideas. This is all completely understandable.

So, why would people join a religious cult? It could be a nurtured and twisted inclination toward abuse and powerlessness—true. But in many cases, it is in fact well intentioned and innate in reason. Cult joiners want a community of people who care for them, look out for them; a sense of mission, to have a shared purpose with a group of people, to be preparing for something or living for something. They want a sense of structure. People join religious cults because they are drawn to a leader who can help them work through lies and give them direction.

Do you see how these reasons I listed are not at all bad reasons? People join cults because they want a better life, order and support. Most are not for sinister reasons. What makes a cult bad is not the reason a person joins, or that they join at all.

What makes a cult bad is who is worshiped by the cult. A cult is ungodly when the allegiance and worship is redirected from Jesus, to a man or woman. This becomes idolatry.

Unless the man is Yeshua, Jesus Christ, the King of kings, this will end badly. No other man should be worshipped and none should want to be.

> A cult is ungodly when the allegiance and worship is redirected from Jesus, to a man or woman. This becomes idolatry.

When a leader is made out to be untouchable, unquestionable and the center of all things, this is how a good-intentioned man turns to evil. He becomes possessive and controlling. A cult is bad because it slowly becomes inwardly focused. They shut the world out and only speak and deal with its members—abuse to the highest degree grows in this environment. An uncorrectable leader and a group of people who are cut off totally from the outside world can be something truly dangerous. When thinking about religious cults, I heard the Lord say to me "There will be more to come." Meaning, the days of religious cults are very real, and not over. Many will spring up as we come nearer to the last days and with that knowledge, God wants something in the earth that addresses the need to have proper leadership with structure and a mission in life—without the abuse and manipulation and evil. We shouldn't cease doing certain good things because evil people have used those very same good elements to draw individuals in and harm them. God is still good and active. And we must trust that He is still creating and moving within His people.

The International House of Prayer, provides what I think is a very helpful list of "7 signs of a true religious cult" (IHOP, 2019):

1. They oppose critical thinking instead of allowing people to think for themselves. Critical thinking is objective—it evaluates information received (not the same as a critical spirit).
2. They dishonor the family unit instead of insisting on the biblical priority of the family unit.
3. They isolate members and reject them for leaving instead of helping them do God's will.
4. They promote inappropriate loyalty and connection to the cult leadership instead of to Jesus.
5. They cross biblical boundaries of behavior instead of walking in purity and integrity.
6. They separate from the Church instead of promoting a culture of honor toward the Church.

7. Emphasizing special revelations that contradict Scripture instead of honoring the Scripture.

This kingdom house model is far from fulfilling the requirements of a cult. If that is not clear, then you may have missed essential points within this book. When the characteristics of the kingdom of God, as outlined in Scripture, are met with the model of a kingdom, then the fruit is life and peace and godliness. In the house model everyone is submitted to the King of kings and are encouraged to have a personal relationship with Him. They are also encouraged to question the leadership and to hold them accountable. Within a house model when someone wants to leave they are released without shame. They are even discipled with the hope that they will grow their own house. The house model is interconnected to the larger body of Christ. The house makes for a stronger and more interconnected church family that knows who they are as a family unit within it, as a company of houses, and who they are as an individual and their role within the house.

This model invites new people to join and when they do they will be joining a royal family. It will be seen and felt based off the language, the care for one another and the emphasis on missional living. The unity of a house family can be like nothing the institutionalize church has ever seen yet on earth. It can, if done right, be even greater than the Medieval days where the family structure and respect for leadership was at its greatest.

"Winter is coming" is a phrase that is said over and over in the Game of Thrones universe. It speaks on the winters that come to Westeros that last for years. It is a phrase that reminds the hearer to prepare for a time of testing under brutal conditions. The winters were a natural time to prepare food, wood, clothing and be strong in mind to survive. The winter is also a reminder of the greater challenge—death zombie creatures coming from beyond the wall. They are whispered to bring an army and wipe out all the living in the whole land. Connection: In Isaiah 61, we also have our own winter coming, it's called deep darkness on the land. I believe the Lord wants us to prepare for the great spiritual battle in end times where the Antichrist will come to deceive all the nations and make them his zombie followers to spiritual death. The Lord wants us to arise and shine, to be ready as these days get colder and darker, to be people of vibrant love. Those that win many people to the Son of Righteousness, escaping the lake of fire, which is the doom of all who do not believe. In light of this coming darkness, get your house in order. Let us gather together for the most epic battle in human history!

Chapter Six

A Final Call

There is a reason why we love stories of kings, lords, princesses and warriors. These stories are shadows to who we are supposed to be. We are seated in Heavenly places with Christ, our big Brother (Romans 8:29; Hebrews 2:11). It is time we arise and shine,

> For your light has come! And the glory of the Lord is risen upon you. (Is 60:1)

> He says He raises the poor out of the dust, *And* lifts the needy out of the ash heap, That He may seat *him* with princes—With the princes of His people. (Psalms 113:7)

Let it be known that the kingdom of darkness is already walking in an order and a respect. This structure makes them powerful and real. Remember when the Tower of Babel was being built, the Lord said if they are not stopped they will be able to accomplish anything (Genesis 11:1-9). When a people are one in mind and have the same language, unity and in order, there is no end to what can be accomplished—good or evil—and the kingdom of darkness is currently walking in that. The evils of this world seem to have no bounds and still to be growing. The kingdom of darkness has no problem walking in the kingdom model which is enforced by manipulation, control, abuse, self-exaltation, back-biting, slander. They remain in order using whatever means is necessary and they are finding success expanding their agenda.

It is time for the Kingdom of Light to get in divine order by the power of the Spirit of God, with all humility, gentleness and servanthood. This is the kingdom order the Lord created. Don't let the darkness do a better job doing kingdom than the ones whose Father created the model. When the Church falls into step, we become an unstoppable force that will see success wherever we go.

> Don't let the darkness do a better job doing kingdom than the ones whose Father created the model.

In the book of Daniel, Daniel has a vision of the courts of heaven. He says, "While I was watching Thrones were set up and the ancient one of days took his seat" (Daniel 7:9). Do you see? Heaven has more than one throne. Yes, there is THE throne and to only Him do we bow. Jesus alone is given all dominion, glory, sovereignty and the authority to rule all people on the earth. But there are other thrones in His courts. I believe, you and I have a throne today, because according to the Scripture we are seated in Heavenly places. If we live as such, we will have a throne to sit on in heaven! We see the thrones of the saints again in the revelation of John.

> And I saw thrones, and they sat on them, and judgment was committed to them. (Revelation 20:4)

In the world, we believe there can be only one king. But in the kingdom of God, there are many kings and queens, all worshiping the One who is, King of kings. I want us to think on our King for a moment. Bear with me. When Jesus was ordered to be crucified, the common practice then was to strip the condemned naked. We may not like it, but we have to be open to the fact that our Lord may not have had any clothes on while on the cross, despite the common image of a piece of cloth covering His loins. In tradition of crucifixion, the point was to completely humiliate the criminal. There is no real reason to think that the Romans would have been any different with this Jewish man. Jesus, in all sense of the word, was "naked". When the soldiers divided His clothes, the only thing the king of the Jews had on was a crown of thorns. Do you see this? The only thing Jesus still had on, while dying for you, was a crown.

This is beyond significant. It is epic imagery, to accompany the most climactic moment in all of history, for all of time. Wearing this painful crown, He purchased ours. He took the crown we deserve, to give us a Crown of Life, Glory and Victory. If we come to the Lord naked like this, that is to say, hiding nothing, like little children, He will give you a crown, an identity, a position in His court. Jesus died to make you royalty, to make you part of His holy family. We may all have different roles but we are one Kingdom.

> The only thing Jesus still had on, while dying for you, was a crown.

God crowned Adam in the garden over the whole of creation. When he sinned, he gave his crown over to Satan. Jesus shows up to give it back to us. He is the greater Adam.

> For if, by the trespass of the one man, death reigned through that one man, how much more will those who receive God's abundant provision of grace and of the gift of righteousness reign in life through the one man, Jesus Christ! Consequently, just as one trespass resulted in condemnation for all people, so also one righteous act resulted in justification and life for all people. (Romans 5:17-18)

Through His sacrifice we are redeemed and alive. Let us not count His sacrifice to small a thing and refuse to walk in the fullness of what He purchased for us—a throne.

> To him who overcomes I will grant to sit with Me on My throne, as I also overcame and sat down with My Father on His throne. (Revelation 3:21)

Jesus' destiny is to share authority with us. He longs for us to arise and shine and come into our fullness. Paul grasped this. He speaks of the saints of old, in Hebrews,

> Therefore, since we are surrounded by so great a cloud of witnesses, let us also lay aside every weight, and sin which clings so closely, and let us run with endurance the race that is set before us... (Hebrews 12:1)

Paul explains that these saints are complete in us.

> And all these, though commended through their faith, did not receive what was promised, since God had provided something better for us, that apart from us they should not be made perfect. (Hebrews 11:39-40)

> Therefore, since we are receiving a kingdom which cannot be shaken, let us have grace, by

which we may serve God acceptably with
reverence and godly fear. (Hebrews 12:28)

Once we are aware that we are seated on a throne
right where we are now we have context to enter into
battle with the enemy more competently. Sitting on the
throne, when we hear the accusations of the enemy
come forth declaring failure and weakness, instead of
sinking low in agreement with these accounts, we can
arise and stand up like a man, or woman, who has an
authoritative voice. You will not be bullied. You will not
be silenced. No, you will declare, "I am a royal child of
God. I am the redeemed of Jesus the Christ, the Lord. I
can literally say to the devil, "I am King Chris the
brilliant, lord of House Rush, son of the Father of lights,
Carrier of the north star, Father to many. "Out of my
presence Flee from me."

Arise

"For your light has come! And the glory of the
Lord is risen upon you" (Is 60:1). It is time to rise
and shine in the face of the world's problems and
declare a solution in Jesus name! To rise and shine
is to take your royal place and speak it out loud and
to make darkness flee from you. Every person in
Christ is important and has a royal duty that they
alone were created to do. So the question is not do
you have a purpose. The question is whether you
will take your position that was bought by the Royal
Blood of Yeshua and become true royals in word
and action. Many believe the lies of the enemy, who

tells us to believe so little of the blood of Jesus that we count ourselves out and never take a seat on the throne.

For those who do take their royal position, and I do hope you do—the Nations will come to your brightness. You will see the world change around you in ways that lets everyone around you know, it is the glory of God having his full way in your life. The Spirit realm will know as well. Every evil, unseen thing, will fear when you rise out of bed in the morning. With the mind of a royal son or daughter, a crown will be seen on your head even when you don't have anything on it. Nothing is impossible for the elect of God. and now is the time to Arise & Shine and show it.

Of the increase of His government and peace There will be no end, Upon the throne of David and over His kingdom, To order it and establish it with judgment and justice From that time forward, even forever. (Isaiah 9:7)

I am only naming what is the call of the Church: arise and shine, as royalty. Christianity will then be known for being a royal family that truly serves one another. A people with power, looking for the New Jerusalem.

When we inherit our eternal home, the New Jerusalem, it will be with Jesus and the true faithful ones who never gave up on a fight of faith will rule and reign with Him, forever. We will increase His government throughout the Universe. Jesus said, "Your kingdom come on the earth as it is in heaven" (Matthew 6:10). So as His kingdom is coming, we are today to take our seat in it. Put on our royal attire, and begin to rule in the midst of our enemies and reign as we serve one another, for the glory of Christ.

May you be challenged and inspired to embrace this truth, that you are the beloved, royal, Ecclesia of God.

Shalom.

Appendix A: Kingdom House Model Sample/House model Bio

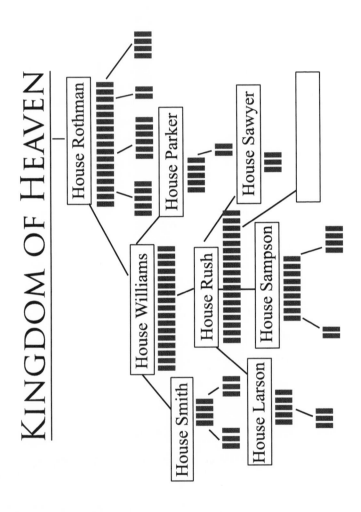

Note. This is a visual of how houses interconnect in service to one another. Reference Chapter Four.

-Signet/Crest   **House Rush Bio**

Tribe: **Levi**

House Motto: **"Arise and Shine"**

House Motto (long): **" Arise and shine for your light has come, and the glory of the Lord is risen upon you. For behold the darkness shall cover the earth and the people but the Lord will arise over you and his glory will been seen upon you.**

We Prepare: **for the darkest hours of human history and for the Lord's return.**

House Psalm: **Psalm 84**

We are stars: **Daniel 12:3**

We are the light of the world: **Matt 5:14**

We are royalty: **1 Peter 2:9, Rev 1:6 Isaiah 62:3**

We walk in the seven spirits of God **- Knowledge -Counsel -Wisdom -Understanding -Strength -Fear of the Lord -Spirit of the LORD**

We are Golden people: **Malachi 3:3**

We will be leaders: **in the New Jerusalem: Rev 3:12**

We are in service to: **House Williams-House Rothman**